LET.
IT.
GO.

LET. IT. GO.

KAREN EHMAN

How to Stop Running the Show
and Start Walking in Faith

ZONDERVAN®

ZONDERVAN.com/
AUTHORTRACKER
follow your favorite authors

ZONDERVAN

Let. It. Go. Study Guide
Copyright © 2012 by Karen Ehman

This title is also available as a Zondervan ebook. Visit www.zondervan.com/ebooks.

Requests for information should be addressed to:

Zondervan, *Grand Rapids, Michigan 49530*

ISBN 978-0-310-68454-1

Cover design and illustrations: Faceout Studios
Interior design: Sarah Johnson and David Conn

Printed in the United States of America

12 13 14 15 16 17 18 19 /DCI/ 20 19 18 17 16 15 14 13 12 11 10 9 8 7 6 5 4 3 2 1

Contents

How to Use This Guide

Group Size

The *Let. It. Go.* video curriculum is designed to be experienced in a group setting such as a Bible study, Sunday school class, or any small group gathering. After viewing each video together, members will participate in a group discussion. Ideally, discussion groups should be no larger than twelve people. You will notice that occasionally there are portions of the discussion where you are encouraged to break into smaller clusters of three to six people each for more heart-to-heart sharing and Scripture study. These times are clearly noted in the guide.

Materials Needed

Each participant should have her own study guide, which includes video outline notes, directions for activities, and discussion questions, as well as a reading plan and personal studies to deepen learning between sessions. Participants are also strongly encouraged to have a copy of the *Let. It. Go.* book. Reading the book alongside the video curriculum provides even deeper insights that make the journey richer and more meaningful (also, a few of the questions pertain to material covered in the book).

Timing

The time notations—for example (16 minutes)—indicate the *actual* time of video segments and the *suggested* time for each activity or discussion.

For example:

Individual Activity: *What Is God Saying to Me?* (3 minutes)

Adhering to the suggested times will enable you to complete each session in one hour. If you have additional time, you may wish to allow more time for discussion and activities, thereby expanding your group's meeting time to an hour and fifteen minutes or an hour and a half.

Facilitation

Each group should appoint a facilitator who is responsible for starting the video and for keeping track of time during discussions and activities. Facilitators may also read questions aloud and monitor discussions, prompting participants to respond and ensuring that everyone has the opportunity to participate.

Between-Sessions Personal Study

Maximize the impact of the course with additional study between group sessions. Carving out about two hours total for personal study between meeting times will enable you to complete both the book and between-session studies by the end of the course. For each session, you may wish to complete the personal study all in one sitting or to spread it out over a few days (for example, working on it a half-hour a day on four different days that week). PLEASE NOTE: If you are unable to finish (or even start!) your between-sessions personal study, still attend the group study video session. We are all busy and life happens. You are still wanted and welcome at class even if you don't have your "homework" done.

Scripture Memory

Each study includes a key Scripture verse that highlights the topic of the session theme. If you wish to maximize your learning experience, you may attempt to memorize these verses. In order to assist you with this goal, all six verses are printed in the back of the study guide.

You may photocopy this page on paper or card stock and then cut out the verses. (You really creative and crafty gals may even want to use scrapbooking paper to layer them on top of some decorative paper).

Then keep them in a handy place—perhaps your car, purse, or laptop bag. You can practice memorizing them when you have times of waiting in the car pool line or at the doctor's office. Or, you may wish to post them at your kitchen sink or on your bathroom mirror where you will see them each day. Laminating them will help to keep them from getting ruined if they get splashed.

It may be helpful to have the group facilitator inquire if any participants are attempting to memorize the key verses. Perhaps those members will want to show up five minutes early (or stay after for a few minutes) to practice reciting them to each other.

God Called and He'd Like His Job Back

Now the serpent was more crafty than any other beast of the field that the Lord God had made. He said to the woman, "Did God actually say …?" (Genesis 3:1 ESV)

Video: *God Called and He'd Like His Job Back* (16 minutes)

Play the video teaching segment for session one. As you watch, record any thoughts or concepts that stand out to you in the notes section below.

Notes

Women have been wired from birth to control. It seems we all inherited the "bossy gene."

At the root of why we over-control is that we don't trust God. We think we know better than he does just what is best for us.

How Eve over-controlled in Genesis 3:1 – 13:

- She was told she could eat of any of the trees in the beautiful Garden of Eden. Well, except for one.
- She listened to Satan's deceptive and crafty words, "Did God *actually* say . . . ?"
- She took matters into her own hands.
- As a result, Eve was tempted with wrong theology.

Cat-and-Dog Theology:

A dog says to its master: "You love me. You feed me. You scratch my neck and rub my belly. You provide for my every need. WOW! *You* must be God."

A cat says to its master: "You love me. You feed me. You scratch my neck and rub my belly. You provide for my every need. WOW! *I* must be God."

This study will feel unfamiliar. Its goes against how we are wired as women to stop running the show and start walking in faith. Although it is not comfortable, it *is* possible.

Group Discussion (10 minutes)

Take a few minutes to discuss what you just watched.

1. What part of the video teaching had the most impact on you?

2. Can you think of an example when a little girl or teenaged young lady exhibited the "bossy gene"? Describe the situation.

3. Brainstorm as a group common areas of life where women love to call the shots. Rattle them off "popcorn" style. Ready? Go!

Cluster Group Discussion (12 minutes)

If your group is comprised of more than twelve members, consider completing this activity in smaller groups of three to six people each.

Turn to Genesis 2:15 – 3:13 and have someone read it aloud. Collaborate to find answers to the following questions as you think about the person of Eve:

- List all of the things that God had provided for Eve in the garden.

- List the worries, if any, Eve would have had living in Paradise.

- Using the version of the Bible you have with you, write out any key words from the description of the serpent in this passage.

- Next, jot down any key words that the serpent said to Eve in their encounter.

- What do you learn from recording these particular words and phrases?

Group Discussion (12 minutes)

Gather back together as one large group and answer the following questions.

4. What is one insight you gained from the small group activity about Eve's life and her encounter with Satan?

5. In many respects, we are modern-day Eves. God has already provided what we need in life, yet Satan still tempts us with wrong thinking. In what areas of life do you most find women questioning God's Word?

6. In the video segment, Karen described the definitions of Cat-and-Dog Theology she learned from the Unveiling Glory ministry. What do you think of these two opposite ways of thinking about God?

7. What makes it so difficult in today's culture to have the proper dog-like theology in life where we allow God to be God and stop trying to do his job for him?

Group Activity (5 minutes)

Time to get the blood circulating!

Near the end of the video segment, Karen asked you to fold your arms the way it felt natural and then to try to fold them in the opposite direction. What did you think of this experiment? Did it feel foreign to you to fold your arms the opposite way?

As a group, do the experiment together again. First, fold your arms the natural-feeling way again. Then, fold them the opposite way once more. Repeat that action quickly five more times. Does it get any easier or do you still have to concentrate as you do it each time?

Leave your arms folded in the opposite, unnatural-feeling position while you answer this next question:

Why does it feel so foreign at times to not be in control? To keep our thoughts to ourselves or hold our opinion? To let someone else in our family or at work make a decision without our input?

(Okay. You can put your arms any way you'd like to now!)

Individual Activity: *What Is God Saying to Me?* (3 minutes)

Complete this activity on your own.

Take a mental inventory of your life. In what areas do you most struggle with wanting your own way or desiring to be in control? Check any that apply:

- ☒ Work situations
- ☒ Husband's behavior
- ☒ Kids' behavior
- ☒ The appearance of the house
- ☒ Extended family situations
- ☒ Others' opinions of me
- ☒ What happens in politics
- ☒ The way others drive
- ☒ How my family members look or dress
- ☒ My appearance
- ☒ Financial matters
- ☒ Other _____

cont.

Now, go back and put a star before the one or two areas where you most feel God may be prompting you to let it go and trust him.

Closing Prayer (2 minutes)

Have one person close in prayer. Then, get ready to learn more in your between-sessions personal study before meeting for session two!

Between-Sessions Personal Study

Read and Learn

Read chapters 1–2 of the *Let. It. Go.* book. Use the space below to record any insights you discovered or questions you may want to bring to the next group session.

Study and Reflect

1. Has there ever been a time in your life when, due to sickness or other circumstances, you were not able to be in control of normal day-to-day activities? If so, describe how that felt.

2. Women wear many hats. We may be a wife, mother, employee, daughter, volunteer, church member, and friend.

   • Think for a moment about your week, keeping in mind those many hats. List them in column one on the chart on the following page.
   • Next, go back and very briefly summarize the primary tasks/ responsibilities associated with each hat. Record these in column two.
   • Finally, on a scale of 1 to 10 (with 1 being "never" and 10 being "always"), how do you rate in each area when it comes to praying to God before launching out to get your tasks accomplished? Record your rating in column three.

I am a:	So, this week I need to:	Rating
Ex.: Mother	Help with homework, pack lunches, carpool	
Ex.: Part-time employee	Work 20 hours	

What do you learn from the above exercise?

While our personalities and methods may vary, our goal is often the same. And I'd wager at the root of our problem are exactly the same two issues I unearthed while confined to my sofa of sickness.

1. We want to feel indispensable.
2. We want to get our own way.

Although these are two common threads, an even stronger similar strand is often woven deep into our "I'll do it my way" souls.

We don't really trust God.

Let. It. Go., page 22

3. Circle the statement which most reflects why you most often try to control.

   I want to feel indispensable.   *I want to get my own way.*

   Reread the statement you circled. Now, explain why you desire for that statement to be true in your life.

4. Which of the following types of controller (described in more detail on pages 20–22 of the *Let. It. Go.* book) do you find most difficult to deal with?

   ☒ The overtly controlling, loud, and outspoken woman
   ☒ The sweet, soft-spoken, but manipulative saint
   ☒ The enabler who constantly covers for others so her family looks good
   ☒ The victim who controls by making you feel sorry for her
   ☒ The people-pleaser who controls because you owe her favors

   Why do you feel it is hard to deal with this type of controller?

   Now (be honest), which one (or more) of these roles do you sometimes assume? Write it below.

   Why do you attempt to control in this way? (Example: my personality type is geared toward this type of control, it has worked for me in the past, etc.)

So, when it comes to a purchase, an activity, an event, a friendship, a hobby, or a pastime, I ask myself, "Is this a tool, a toy, or a tangent?"

Let. It. Go., page 39

5. In *Let. It. Go.*, Karen encourages us to ask ourselves with each purchase, activity, event, friendship, hobby, or pastime, "Is this a tool, a toy, or a tangent?" A tool helps us effectively live life. A toy helps us relax and enjoy life. A tangent knocks us off course and causes us to waste time, energy, and/or money on a trivial activity that does nothing for our life. List any areas of your life that, if left unchecked, can easily morph into a tangent. (Example: social media, television, scrapbooking, etc.)

6. Look up the following Bible passages. After each, write how it speaks to the concept of time-wasting tangents.

- Psalm 31:14–15

- Romans 12:1–2

- Ephesians 5:15–17

- Colossians 3:17

Now, based on what you just read in Scripture, what are some questions you can ask yourself that will help you to avoid time-wasting tangents in your life?

Scripture Memory Verse of the Week

Each week of our study will feature a verse to ponder and even memorize if you desire. For your convenience, all verses are printed out in the back of this study guide. You may photocopy that page on cardstock or colored paper. Then, cut out the verses and place them in a prominent place — purse, dashboard, desk, kitchen sink — where you can read and study them regularly. (You may want to laminate them if posting them at your kitchen sink. Been there. Splashed that.)

Here is our verse for this week:

Now the serpent was more crafty than any other beast of the field that the LORD God had made. He said to the woman, "Did God actually say ...?"

Genesis 3:1 (ESV)

Combating the "Me First" Mentality

A [self-confident] fool has no delight in understanding but only in revealing his personal opinions *and* himself. (Proverbs 18:2 AMP)

Checking In (10 minutes)

Welcome to session two of *Let. It. Go.* An important part of this study is sharing what you have learned from reading the book and from completing your between-sessions personal study. Remember, don't worry if you didn't cover all of the material. You are still welcome at the study and your input is valuable!

- What from the session one video segment most challenged or encouraged you since the group last met together?
- What insights did you discover from your reading of chapters 1 – 2 of the *Let. It. Go.* book?
- What stood out to you from the questions and activities in the between-sessions personal study?

Video: *Combating the "Me First" Mentality* (20 minutes)

Play the video teaching segment for session two. As you watch, record any thoughts or concepts that stand out to you in the notes section below.

Notes

Sometimes we wish we had "do-overs" in life so we could go back and choose a better outcome for ourselves.

We control because we have a "me first" mentality. We put ourselves before others and sometimes even before God.

Genesis 11 – 22 tells the story of the impatient princess Sarai turned mother/princess Sarah. Sarai was unable to have children so she sought a remedy herself by coming up with a plan.

Sarai did something that was a common cultural practice but was not what God had intended for her.

Eventually God changed Sarai's name to Sarah. Later, she is absent from the account of Abraham attempting to offer Isaac as a sacrifice. Perhaps Sarah finally learned to stop taking matters into her own hands and start trusting God instead.

What can we learn from Sarai/Sarah's story?

• Take God at his word, but also trust his timing.

• Don't be a "me first" maniac.

• Don't behave in a way that makes you desire "do-overs" in life. But when you do, allow God to turn your predicament into purpose.

Group Discussion (10 minutes)

Take a few minutes to discuss what you just watched.

1. What part of the teaching had the most impact on you?

2. In what areas of life are we most tempted to want "do-overs"?

3. How is our desire to do over connected to wanting to put ourselves first?

Cluster Group Discussion (5 minutes)

If your group is comprised of more than twelve members, consider completing this discussion in smaller groups of three to six people each.

4. In what ways do we modern-day women tend to be like the impatient Sarai? Offer a specific example.

5. In what area of your life are you the most impatient and find it hardest to trust God's timing?

Group Discussion (10 minutes)

Gather back together as one large group and answer the following questions.

6. Discuss your reactions to the following statements from the video.

   • Take God at his word, but also trust his timing.

   • Don't be a "me first" maniac, not only in getting your way but in expressing your opinion. (Have someone read Proverbs 18:2 aloud before you answer this one.)

   • Don't behave in a way that makes you want "do-overs" in life. But, when you do, let God turn your predicament into purpose.

7. What common cultural practices do women turn to today that might not be God's best for them?

8. Read 1 Peter 3:5–7. Rather than being known as an impatient control freak, what is Sarah's legacy?

Having an imperfect spouse keeps me on my knees. If I had a perfect husband who could meet my every need, I would have no need for God. That is why I am thankful I have a husband who drives me nuts (and he a wife who drives him even nuttier) because ... it drives us both straight to Jesus.

Let. It. Go. video

Individual Activity: *What Is God Saying to Me?* (3 minutes)

Complete this activity on your own.

How do you hope your children or others in your life will remember you when it comes to your relationship with God? Take a moment to jot a few sentences that spell that out.

How can learning to stop trying to control and start trusting God and his timing help this wish to come true?

Closing Prayer (2 minutes)

Have one person close the group in prayer. Then, get ready to learn more in your between-sessions personal study prior to session three!

Between-Sessions Personal Study

Read and Learn

Read chapters 3–4 of the *Let. It. Go.* book. Use the space below to record any insights you discovered or questions you may want to bring to the next group session.

Study and Reflect

1. Besides the story of the meddling mother Wanda Holloway, are there any other stories from the news headlines that you can think of that showcase a woman's runaway desire for control?

2. Turn to pages 48–49 of the *Let. It. Go.* book and review the interaction between Eve and the serpent. Fill in the missing words below:

   Step #1: Satan hissed, hurling _____ Eve's way and causing her to _____ God's plan and to _____ his _____.

   Step #2: Eve didn't _____ _____ to God's _____.

   Step #3: Satan _____ _____.

   Step #4: Eve _____ _____.

   Can you think of a situation in your own life (or in the life of someone close to you) where Satan used similar tactics? Briefly jot the situation below noting how it is similar to any of the steps above.

Our only solution is to cultivate the gentle art of acceptance, of learning not to ask "Why me?" but rather "What am I supposed to learn at this junction of life that will make me a better person and draw me closer to God?"

Let. It. Go., **page 53**

3. Name a situation in your life right now where you wish God would move a little more quickly. Describe it in the space below.

Now, even though it may be difficult, list one or two blessings that might come from God continuing to take his time in answering your request or remedying the situation. (Hint: What character qualities is he growing in you?)

4. Turn to the statements and the corresponding Bible verses on pages 56–58 of *Let. It. Go.* Pick two or three of the "When I'm tempted to think" statements that most often pop into your mind and write them out in the space provided below.

1.

2.

3.

cont.

Now, for each of the above statements, give your rationale for thinking it at times. Don't try to clean up your words or be overly spiritual. Give your honest (even if fleshly) reasons that you sometimes feel that way. Write your reasons in the numbered spaces below (corresponding to the numbers of the statements above).

1.

2.

3.

Finally, go back to the book and read the verse that was given in the corresponding "Be reminded that God says . . ." section for each of the statements you chose above. Read each one slowly, allowing their truths to sink in.

How can the corresponding verses help to renew your mind and align it with God's way of thinking?

In the original Hebrew, the phrase that is translated "Your desire shall be for your husband," actually means that a woman's desire would be for her husband's position. Meaning, he would be the pants-wearer in the family, but she would want to wiggle her sweet little self into them instead and leave him holding a fig leaf. When I strung those two thought patterns together, the mysterious Scripture verse finally made sense.

Let. It. Go., page 68

5. If you are married, in what areas do you struggle with wanting to be in control in your relationship? (Example: finances, vacation decisions, home improvement projects, etc.)

How do you and your husband usually handle differences of opinion in these areas when they arise?

6. Consider the following statements from pages 73–77 of the *Let. It. Go.* book. Check the one that most speaks to you in your current marriage situation.

☒ Realize the act of submitting is always a choice by and action of the wife.
☒ Know that backing off and not controlling your husband will feel very foreign.
☒ Next, recognize the subtle difference between manipulation and influence.
☒ Then, find the unique dance steps that work for your marriage.
☒ Recognize when you need dance lessons from a pro.

Why did you check the statement that you did? What do you feel God is saying to you about that specific concept?

cont.

Write out a two- or three-sentence prayer to God about this topic. Openly pour your heart out to him.

Scripture Memory Verse of the Week

Here is our verse for this week to ponder, study, and even memorize, if desired. (Remember, all the memory verses are printed out for you in the back of this study guide. You may photocopy them for your convenience.)

A [self-confident] fool has no delight in understanding but only in revealing his personal opinions *and* himself.

Proverbs 18:2 (AMP)

Pursuing the Appearance of Perfection

She opens her mouth with wisdom, and the teaching of kindness is on her tongue. (Proverbs 31:26 ESV)

Checking In (7 minutes)

Welcome to session three of *Let. It. Go.* An important part of this study is sharing what you have learned from reading the book and from completing your between-sessions personal study. Remember; don't worry if you didn't cover all of the material. You are still welcome at the study and your input is valuable!

- What from the session two video segment most challenged or encouraged you since the group last met? Anyone have a chance to combat the "me first" mentality in a real-life situation?

- What insights did you discover from your reading of chapters 3–4 of the *Let. It. Go.* book?

- What did you find interesting or challenging in the between-sessions personal study?

Video: *Pursuing the Appearance of Perfection* (23 minutes)

Play the video segment for session three. As you watch, record any thoughts or concepts that stand out to you in the notes section below.

Notes

Are you ever a control freak about your house or the actions of someone who lives there?

Why at times do you get frustrated with others in your home when they carry out certain tasks? Because they failed to do it your way.

Sometimes we over-control because we are pursuing the appearance of perfection and perfection, to us, is having things done our way.

The woman in Proverbs 31 was often cited for her "doing." Let's look instead at her "being."

She was a woman who didn't pursue the appearance of perfection but was pursuing the person and purposes of God.

How can we go from pursuing perfection (or wanting things done our way) to speaking with wisdom and kindness? Let's ask ourselves these questions:

- "Does it matter now?"
- "Will it matter tomorrow?"
- "Will it affect eternity?"
- "Is God trying to teach *me* something? If so, what?"
- "Can I pause and praise instead of interrupt and instigate?"
- "Is there really an issue here that needs addressing with my child (spouse)?"
- "Am I just being a control freak and need to let it go?"

Strategies for being more "Proverbs 31 woman" and less "Tin Pot dictator":

- Remember, there are lots of ways to get to four.

- Recognize the difference between goals and desires.

- Recognize that imperfect can still make perfectly wonderful memories.

Group Discussion (10 minutes)

Take a few minutes to discuss what you just watched.

1. What part of the teaching had the most impact on you?

2. Of the questions in the video notes that Karen challenged us to ask ourselves when we are frustrated with the way someone is performing a task around the house, which most stood out to you?

3. In what areas of your home or family life would it benefit you to remember that "there are lots of ways to get to four"?

4. Why do you think we so often feel that things around the house must be done the way we normally do them? What might be at the core of feeling this way?

5. Can you name a time in your life when imperfect still made a perfectly wonderful memory?

Cluster Group Discussion (10 minutes)

If your group is comprised of more than twelve members, consider completing this discussion in smaller groups of three to six people each.

6. Skim Proverbs 31 and jot down your answers to these questions, making note of what verses you found them in:

   What are some actions this woman took or tasks she performed.

   What might have been her motives for doing these things?

   What other people are mentioned besides the woman in this passage? List how they benefited from her actions or what they thought or said about her.

   For fun, have your group come up with a first name for this woman. Be ready to give the larger group the reason why you chose that particular name.

Group Discussion (5 minutes)

Gather back together as one large group and answer the following questions.

7. What name did your cluster group give this biblical gal and why? (Take turns sharing your answers.)

8. What new insights did you gain from this session's study of the unnamed woman in Proverbs 31.

Individual Activity: *What Is God Saying to Me?* (3 minutes)

Complete this activity on your own.

Ask God to bring to mind a time when you did *not* speak with wisdom and kindness on your tongue with a family member or coworker. List the person's name below and briefly describe the situation.

Spend a minute searching your heart asking God if you need to go to this person to ask his or her forgiveness. If God says yes, then write below how and when you will do this. (Example: apologize in person, write a personal note, call tomorrow, send a text as soon as this study is over.)

Closing Prayer (2 minutes)

Have one person close in prayer. Don't forget to contact the person (or persons) God put on your heart in the individual activity. Then, get ready for your between-sessions personal study prior to session four.

Between-Sessions Personal Study

Read and Learn

Read chapters 5–6 of the *Let. It. Go.* book. Use the space below to record any insights you discovered, concepts that challenged you, or questions you may want to bring to the next group session.

Study and Reflect

1. In what ways are parents pressured to have perfect children? (Examples: public behavior, academics, sports.)

2. Has there ever been a time when you personally felt the pressure to mother "perfectly" because of the watchful eyes of friends or family members? Or, if you do not have children, can you think of a time from your childhood when you were expected to display exemplary behavior? Describe that time in the space below.

But with any correction I have to ask myself, "What is the point?"

Am I trying to nip a destructive pattern or behavior?

Good.

Am I attempting to teach them to respect the authority in their life, which for now is their parents, so that one day they will respect their boss or the government or the police officer?

Excellent.

Am I trying to teach them diligence, patience, the value of hard work or honesty?

Wonderful.

But I also have to ask myself this, "Is this really a neutral issue and I'm just trying to control my child and get my own way? AM I hurting my child (physically or emotionally) because of my own needs?"

BINGO!

Let. It. Go., page 90

3. For each of the following pairs of statements, circle the one which best describes your parenting style.

I want to control who my kids' friends are.	I trust my kids to make their own choice in friendships.
I micromanage my kids to ensure their schoolwork gets done.	I let my kids tackle their schoolwork themselves and deal with the results.
I try to be in control of my children's athletic performance.	I let my kids decide what sports to play and how often to practice them outside of officially scheduled practice times.

I push my kids to excel in musical or other extracurricular activities.	I let my kids join and participate in such activities according to their own interests and desires.
I want to have control over my children's appearances.	I let my kids select their own clothing, makeup, or hairstyles as long as they aren't offensive or immodest.
I exert control over my kids' screen time (television, computer, video games).	I let my kids call the shots when it comes to activities that involve a screen.
I often correct my children's speech.	If my kids misspeak, I keep my own mouth shut.
I attempt to make sure my kids are reading their Bibles, attending church, and growing their relationship with God.	I am "hands off" when it comes to the spiritual lives of my offspring.

4. Part of being a parent does include guiding and — to a point — controlling your children's behavior until they are old enough to make sound choices on their own. Of the eight areas covered in question 3, which do you feel are ones where parents can relinquish control rather early and let kids make their own decisions? Give reasons for your answer(s).

Which are areas where a parent should hold firmer control until the kids are closer to adulthood? Why?

When giving instruction, it appears that this woman in the Hall of Fame of Scripture was careful to speak in a way that honored and glorified God. The Amplified Version, verse 26, rendered as close to the original language as possible, reads, "She opens her mouth in skillful and godly Wisdom, and on her tongue is the law of kindness [giving counsel and instruction]."

Kindness.

The kind of tone of voice you'd use with a stranger.

Friendly, not feisty.

And "giving counsel."

Counsel is giving advice and guidance in a gentle but direct way that helps the person seeking the instructions.

Counsel is not barking.

Counsel is not belittling.

Counsel is not superlatives like "Why can't you ever ...?" and "See, you never ...!"

Yes, we should be conscientious, giving counsel; but we should not be controlling, or complaining with criticism.

Let. It. Go., **pages 117–118**

Feisty Friendly
5. On a scale of 1–10, when it comes to being feisty or friendly in your home, where do you usually land?

1   2   3   4   5   6   7   8   9   10

FEISTY   FRIENDLY

Next, think about your interaction with coworkers, neighbors, or church members. Where do you usually fall on the same scale?

1 2 3 4 5 6 7 8 9 10
FEISTY   FRIENDLY

Finally, what about your dealings with complete strangers such as the grocery store clerk, bank teller, or dental receptionist?

1 2 3 4 5 6 7 8 9 10
FEISTY   FRIENDLY

6. Review the continuums from question 5. What do you discover?

Are there any changes you would like to make about your feisty/friendly tendencies and tones with those in your home? Record them here.

7. Grab a Bible, bring up a Bible app on your smart phone, or log on to an online Bible reading site such as *www.biblegateway.com*. Read the following verses and jot down any key words or phrases in the space provided.

- Job 6:24

- Psalm 34:12–14

- Psalm 64:3

cont.

- Psalm 139:4

- Proverbs 15:1–2

- Proverbs 21:23

- James 1:26

8. What stands out the most to you from these verses? Write out a sentence prayer to God about your tongue based on what you discovered and record it here.

Scripture Memory Verse of the Week

Here is our verse for this week to ponder, study, and even memorize, if desired. (Remember, all the memory verses are printed out for you in the back of this study guide. You may photocopy them for your convenience.)

She opens her mouth with wisdom, and the teaching of kindness is on her tongue.

Proverbs 31:26 (ESV)

Practicing the Art of Soul Control

Truly my soul silently waits for God; from Him comes my salvation. He only is my rock and my salvation; He is my defense; I shall not be greatly moved. (Psalm 62:1–2 NKJV)

Checking In (9 minutes)

Welcome to session four of *Let. It. Go.* An important part of this study is sharing what you have learned from reading the book and from completing your between-sessions personal study. Remember, don't worry if you didn't cover all of the material. You are still welcome at the study and your input is valuable!

- What from the session three video segment most challenged or encouraged you since the group last met? Any chance to practice "speaking with wisdom and kindness" on your tongue?
- What insights did you discover from your reading of chapters 5–6 of the *Let. It. Go.* book?
- What most spoke to you from the between-sessions personal study?

Video: *Practicing the Art of Soul Control* (21 minutes)

Play the video segment for session four. As you watch, record any thoughts or concepts that stand out to you in the notes section below.

Notes

Sometimes situations in life occur that rattle our souls.

Many times in the Psalms, the writers used the word *Selah*, which means "to pause and listen" or "to stop and think of that."

The psalmists also often used the expression "My soul" or "Oh my soul" when writing, making it appear that they were talking not only to God or to others, but to themselves.

Sometimes we have to do what Karen's friend Renee Swope calls "bossing my heart around."

David learned the fine art of soul control:

- Soul control is when we speak God's truth to ourselves.

- Soul control is when we recognize that life is not fair, that others prosper who seem evil while the righteous seem to flail about.

- Soul control is when we pause to remember our place. And God's.

- Soul control is learning to idle our brain before we engage our mouth, thereby saving ourselves a boatload of heartache, wounded relationships, and regret.

- Soul control is when we stop—sometimes midsentence—and realign our thinking and resulting actions with God's Word.

- Soul control is when we finally realize that it is only God who has *sole* control over the universe. We do not. And even though it appears that sometimes people or even Satan control the situation, they do not.

- Soul control is a fresh dose of perspective amidst the turmoil of life that can transform a control freak woman (who has only wounded with her words perhaps, but killed nonetheless) into a woman who, like transformed David, follows hard after God's heart.

• Soul control not only changes us. It can change others.

When we can't control our circumstances, we must learn to control our soul.

Group Discussion (10 minutes)

Take a few minutes to discuss what you just watched.

1. What part of the teaching had the most impact on you?

2. Can you think of a time when you had to "boss your heart around" and practice the fine art of soul control? Share briefly with the group the situation and your thought patterns surrounding it.

3. Which of the video note statements about soul control do you most need to remember at this point in your life and why?

Cluster Group Discussion (10 minutes)

If your group is comprised of more than twelve members, consider completing this discussion in smaller groups of three to six people each.

4. Have a person read aloud the following verses one at a time. After each verse is read, discuss what you learn about talking to your own soul from the verse. Record your findings in the spaces provided:

   • Psalm 42:11

   • Psalm 43:5

   • Psalm 62:5

   • Psalm 84:2

   • Psalm 94:19

Group Discussion (5 minutes)

Gather back together as one large group and answer the following questions.

5. Have the cluster groups take turns summarizing what they discovered from the verses in Psalms about controlling our souls.

6. In what practical ways can we learn to take the anxious thoughts that invade our minds and turn them into prayers? (Example: When Karen wanted to over-control her daughter's choice to travel in bad weather, she could have turned her fretful concerns into a prayer that God would both protect her daughter and teach her something she might never learn if not allowed to make her own choices and mistakes.)

Individual Activity: What Is God Saying to Me? (3 minutes)

Complete this activity on your own.

Ask God to bring to your mind a situation or person over which you have a hard time giving up control. Write about that circumstance or individual here.

Now, pen a prayer — speaking to God and to your own soul — about this in an attempt to practice the fine art of soul control.

Closing Prayer (2 minutes)

Have one person close the group in prayer. Then, get ready for your between-sessions personal study time prior to the next meeting.

Between-Sessions Personal Study

Read and Learn

Read chapters 7–9 of the *Let. It. Go.* book. Use the space below to record any insights you discovered or questions you may want to bring to the next group session. (Yes friends, three chapters this week. But don't fret. So not as to overload you and put you in a time crunch, there aren't as many questions as usual.)

Study and Reflect

1. What most often frustrates you about your current schedule? Is there not enough down time due to a packed agenda? Perhaps it is having multiple family members going in different directions as you try to sync their travel. Or, maybe you have lots of time on your hands but are a poor manager of it. Write your greatest challenge here.

2. Read Proverbs 16:9. What part does being in control play in managing our time? After all, we can't simply sit idly by and expect tasks to perform themselves, right? Describe what you feel is a fair balance of control and acceptance when it comes to attempting to manage time, knowing that we may face crises, delays, and interruptions.

Whether your life contains life-altering crises, out-of-control circumstances, or relatively normal bumps and blips, you must nestle yourself neatly and surrendered into the spot God has reserved for you in it all.

You can't always change your circumstances.

You can change your attitude.

You shouldn't seek to micromanage.

You should seek to trust God.

Instead of longing for God to change the trajectory of your life's storyline, look for his face as you practice your faith at each twist and turn along the way.

Yes, you can't change the weather. But you can grab an umbrella.

Let. It. Go., pages 165–166

3. In chapter eight of Let. It. Go. we encounter the Old Testament character Queen Esther, an excellent example of a strong woman who knew how to control what she could, trust God with what she couldn't and, most importantly, decide which was which. Of the statements below suggesting lessons we can learn from her (also found on pages 163–165 of Let. It. Go.), which one most resonates with you and why?

- *Remember God is God and you are not.*
- *Pray, and if you must, fast.*
- *Solicit spiritual help.*
- *Do what you can.*
- *Don't do what you can't.*
- *Decide where to glance and where to gaze.*
- *Know when to move and when to stay put.*

4. On page 177 of *Let. It. Go.*, Karen writes about people pulling "the God card," in other words, trying to control your actions or opinions by telling you "God laid this on my heart," or "The Lord told me to tell you," etc. Have you ever had someone try this tactic with you? If so, briefly describe what happened.

Just as we often encourage our teens to have words ready to speak for a time when they are offered drugs or alcohol, we can be ready to respond to controlling people who try to manipulate us by invoking the name of the Almighty. In the future, what might you say to someone attempting to play "the God card" with you?

What transformed David from a control freak that would stop short of nothing to get his own way — even murdering a man so he could take his wife (See 2 Samuel 11) — into a man who was known as someone who was after God's very heart?

I think it's because he learned the fine art of soul control.

Let. It. Go., page 183

5. Read the following verses and after each record what you learn about controlling your soul when you can't control your circumstances.

- Psalm 103:1–2

- Psalm 116:7–8

- Psalm 130:5

- Psalm 143:8

If we want to guard our hearts and minds, we have to immerse ourselves in truth. We do that by opening God's Word and letting God's Word open us. That's how we are made new in the attitude of our minds.

Lysa TerKeurst, *Unglued*, pages 145–146

Scripture Memory Verse of the Week

Here is our verse for this week to ponder, study, and even memorize, if desired. (Remember, all the memory verses are printed out for you in the back of this study guide. You may photocopy them for your convenience.)

Truly my soul silently waits for God; from Him comes my salvation. He only is my rock and my salvation; He is my defense; I shall not be greatly moved.

Psalm 62:1–2 (NKJV)

When Comparisons Lead to Over-Control

For I have learned how to be content (satisfied to the point where I am not disturbed or disquieted) in whatever state I am. (Philippians 4:11 AMP)

Checking In (9 minutes)

Welcome to session 5 of *Let. It. Go.* An important part of this study is sharing what you have learned from reading the book and from completing your between-sessions personal study. Remember, don't worry if you didn't cover all of the material. You are still welcome at the study and your input is valuable!

- Think back to the session four video segment. Did you have a chance to practice the art of "soul control" in any situation since the group last met?

- What insights did you discover from your reading of chapters 7–9 of the *Let. It. Go.* book?

- What most jumped out at you from the between-sessions personal study?

- Do you have any questions for the group?

Video: *When Comparisons Lead to Over-Control* (24 minutes)

Play the video segment for session five. As you watch, record any thoughts or concepts that stand out to you in the notes section below.

Notes

Comparisons kill our contentment. We are all usually content with our own red Schwinn hand-me-down bike until we spy our neighbor riding by on her brand new, bright blue Mud Puppy.

When we allow comparisons to kill our contentment, we kick into control.

Rachel and Leah fell into the comparison trap and began to dwell in the land of "must be nice." Leah had children, but what she really wanted was to feel loved and pretty. Rachel was loved and pretty, but what she really wanted was to have children.

Why do we often come up short when we compare? Because we compare our reality to another person's appearance.

In the Greek, the word in Philippians 4:11 rendered *content* means "to be satisfied to the point where I am no longer disturbed or disquieted."

It is always best to be an original version of yourself than a cheap imitation of someone else.

When we decide to stop letting comparisons kill our contentment, we will secure ourselves a one-way ticket out of the land of "must be nice."

Group Discussion (12 minutes)

Take a few minutes to discuss what you just watched.

1. What part of the teaching had the most impact on you?

2. Karen mentioned many areas where women let comparisons kill their contentment—possessions, looks, income, personality, marital status. Which of these do you observe most often as you survey our current culture?

   With which of these do you most struggle in your own life? Explain.

3. In the video teaching segment, Karen states that our mothers and grandmothers only saw the "Joneses" a few times a week at most. Now they parade before our eyes daily in a steady stream on the Internet. What part do you feel the Internet and social media play in tempting women to live in the land of "must be nice" as they observe what is happening in the lives of others?

Cluster Group Discussion (5 minutes)

If your group is comprised of more than twelve members, consider completing this discussion in smaller groups of three to six people each.

4. Have one person read aloud Philippians 4:11–13. Paul stated that he had learned to be content in virtually opposite situations—whether well-fed or hungry, living in plenty or in want. Brainstorm as a group opposite situations we modern women might face

wherein we need to cultivate contentment. For example: "Whether I struggle with infertility or pop out babies in rapid succession." Record those statements below and have one person be ready to share them with the full group.

Group Discussion (5 minutes)

Gather back together as one large group and answer the following questions.

5. Have someone from each cluster group share their group's statements from question 4.

6. Have you ever known someone whose circumstances seemed less-than-lovely, yet was content anyway? What was the person's situation? Why do you think he or she was able to experience contentment despite the circumstances?

Individual Activity: *What Is God Saying to Me?* (3 minutes)

Complete this activity on your own.

Take a moment to get alone in your thoughts, quiet before the Lord. Ask him to reveal to you the one area in your life where you most struggle with comparisons. Write briefly about it here.

Now, in your own sweet handwriting, copy these words from Philippians 4:13 (NKJV), but don't put a period at the end of the sentence. Instead, add the words "even when it comes to" and then craft a phrase about the situation you just wrote down to finish your sentence.

I can do all things through Christ who strengthens me.

Closing Prayer (2 minutes)

Have one person close the group in prayer. Then, break for the week to tackle the final portion of between-sessions personal study. The next time the group meets will be the final teaching segment. Sniff, sniff. Enjoy your time between sessions!

Between-Sessions Personal Study

Read and Learn

Read chapters 10–11 of the *Let. It. Go.* book and record any thoughts or insights you discovered in the space provided.

The more we compare ourselves to other women, the higher our expectations are set and something known as the "Perfection Infection" sets in.

Jill Savage, *No More Perfect Moms*

Study and Reflect

1. Karen writes about unearthing her diary from sixth grade and discovering how even as a young teen, she wanted to be someone else. Think back to your own sixth-grade self. In what areas of life were you envious of others?

   Was there anyone in particular that you wished you were more like? Who and why?

2. Read the following verses and record your thoughts on the light they shed on comparisons in the spaces provided after each one.

   • Proverbs 14:30

- Proverbs 27:4

- Ecclesiastes 4:4

- James 3:14

- 1 Peter 2:1

Ask any seasoned turf grass specialist (I'm related to one), and they will tell you this truth. The grass actually has the best chance of turning out Kermit-the-Frog green when it's frequently fertilized and habitually hydrated, and when the pesky, deep-rooted, and often recurring weeds are intentionally pulled out. That's where you'll discover the softest, greenest, thickest grass of all.

Let. It. Go., pages 193–194

3. Think about the situation where you most struggle with comparisons that you wrote down in the session five individual activity. (Or, if you haven't thought of one, do so now.) Got it?

Now, as you consider this life circumstance, answer the following questions. Please take your time as you respond to these important perspective-gaining ponderings. Perhaps you will want to do this over two or more days between sessions.

- What does God want me to learn about him that I might never discover if he were to suddenly pluck me out of this situation?

cont.

- What Christlike character traits is he trying to grow in me — patience, trust, compassion, faith?

- Who is watching — either up close or from afar — and discovering what God is like by my reactions to my current situation?

- How might my empathy for others deepen if I go through this current trial with grace and acceptance?

- What is God trying to say to me, not by the outcome, but through the voyage?

4. In the space below, craft a heartfelt prayer to God about your various answers in question 3. Be honest. Be real. Ask him to shift your perspective in the situation and make you more like Jesus because of the circumstance you are dealing with.

Scripture Memory Verse of the Week

Here is our verse for this week to ponder, study, and even memorize, if desired. (Remember, all the memory verses are printed out for you in the back of this study guide. You may photocopy them for your convenience.)

For I have learned how to be content (satisfied to the point where I am not disturbed or disquieted) in whatever state I am.

Philippians 4:11 (AMP)

Fixing Your Eyes on the Attitude Indicator

So, we are always confident and know that while we are at home in the body we are away from the Lord. For we walk by faith, not by sight. (2 Corinthians 5:6–7 HCSB)

Checking In (5 minutes)

Welcome to the final session of *Let. It. Go.* An important part of this study is sharing what you have learned from reading the book and from completing your between-sessions personal study. Remember, don't worry if you didn't cover all of the material. You are still welcome at the study and your input is valuable!

- What from the session five video segment most challenged or encouraged you since the group last met? Were you tempted to compare yourself or your circumstances with someone else? Were you able to respond differently this time than you normally do?

- What insights did you discover from your reading of chapters 10 – 11 of the *Let. It. Go.* book?

- What did you get out of the between-sessions personal study?

Video: *Fixing Our Eyes on the Attitude Indicator* (25 minutes)

Play the video segment for session six. As you watch, record any thoughts or concepts that stand out to you in the notes section below.

Notes

There are two ways to fly an airplane:

- Visual Flight Rules (VFR) = flying by sight in clear, daytime conditions

- Instrumental Flight Rules (IFR) = flying by the instrument panel because sight is limited

The attitude indicator

Controlled Flight Into Terrain (CFIT)

In the Old Testament, Joseph was a man who kept his attitude in check even when life grew dark.

Joseph's attitude can be summed up in these two phrases: Don't be God. Do be nice.

An old nautical proverb states: "Enslave yourself to the chart and the compass and gain the freedom of the seas. The rest must sail close to the shore."

In our spiritual life, we walk by faith, not by sight (2 Corinthians 5:7). Our chart is the Bible. Our compass is the Holy Spirit.

Trying to be in control of everyone and everything is not a godly pursuit. When we do it, we aren't trying to be godly, we are trying to be God. That is what got Satan kicked out of heaven.

Whatever challenge you are facing now where you are tempted to step in and control things, remember this truth: God is not worried.

In order to get a grip in life, you have got to let go.

Group Discussion (8 minutes)

Take a few minutes to discuss what you just watched.

1. What part of the teaching had the most impact on you?

2. When we try to "fly" in life based upon sight, what types of indicators do we watch for? (Examples: the approval of others, monetary success, etc.)

3. Why is it so difficult to walk in faith when we can't see the entire picture or know the final outcome?

4. How is it true spiritually that if we enslave ourselves to the "chart" (Bible) and "compass" (Holy Spirit), we can gain the freedom of the seas and not have to sail close to the shore?

Cluster Group Discussion (10 minutes)

If your group is comprised of more than twelve members, consider completing this discussion in smaller groups of three to six people each.

5. Take turns reading aloud the various verses in Genesis below. After each passage is read, list the difficulties Joseph faced in his life.

   • Genesis 37:4 – 5; 23 – 28

   • Genesis 39:1, 6 – 20a

   In these unfair situations, what could Joseph have done or said in his own defense?

6. How *did* Joseph react to these unfair situations? Read the following verses to compile your answer.

   • Genesis 39:2 – 5
   • Genesis 39:20b – 23
   • Genesis 41:1 – 16

   What was the result of Joseph's God-honoring attitude? Read Genesis 41:41 – 46.

Group Discussion (10 minutes)

Gather back together as one large group and answer the following questions.

7. What do you most want to remember about your cluster group study of Joseph and his attitude?

8. Think back to your life before you started this study. On a scale of 1–10 (with 1 being "never" and 10 being "always"), what number would you have given yourself when it comes to how often you trusted God rather than tried to control situations yourself? Has that number changed at all? Or, do you have a desire to see that number change? Explain.

9. Of the characters addressed in this study — Eve, Sarah, the Proverbs 31 woman, David, Rachel, Leah, and Joseph — to whom do you most relate and why?

10. Briefly review the notes you took in this guide and be ready to share one aspect of the study that really spoke to you. Then take a few moments for those who wish to share their insight.

Closing Prayer (2 minutes)

Have one person close the group in prayer, thanking God for the work he has done and the growth he has caused in each of your lives.

Final Personal Study

If we want to be free from fear and walk in faith, we must hold onto what God has taught us, replacing our ways with His. We will only overcome our fears by walking through them, holding God's hand, and trusting God's heart to lead, protect, and preserve us.

Renee Swope, *A Confident Heart*, page 197

Study and Reflect

1. Take the next few days to think about the many areas in which you may be tempted to try to run the show rather than walk in faith. Choosing just one or two areas per day from the list that follows, write out your goals in the form of an honest prayer to God about each area. Be specific, mentioning people or situations where you are tempted to over-control and not trust him.

   • Marriage

   • Mothering

   • Finances

   • Work situations

- Schedule

- Extended family

- Friends

- Health

- Home

- Life circumstances

- Situations and choices of loved ones

Yes, it is true: the out-of-control life is a refreshingly thrilling ride. When we relinquish control, let go and "let God," we find our faith and the cadence of life that notices the small and the beauty in all.

Will you try it?

cont.

Will you trust God?

Will you stop running the show and start walking in faith?

Will you loosen your grip on life and grab tight the edge of his garment? He will see and respond. He indeed can heal us all of our misplaced grasping for things that are not ours to decide, or ours to do or to have. If we but lean hard into his loving arms and find our safe and secure place, we can discover the thrill of being both completely out of control and smack-dab in the center of his will — the adventure of the relinquished life.

Let. It. Go., pages 216–217

2. Think about your overall attitude after experiencing this study for the past six sessions. Has your desire to control people and circumstances changed at all? How about your longing to trust God rather than take matters into your own hands?

    On the continuum below, place an X on the place you feel was most reflective of your perspective BEFORE starting this study. Then, place a cross where you feel your heart is now. Not necessarily your actions. Change doesn't happen overnight. Just place the cross where your heart longs to be.

    ●━━━━━━━━━━━━━━━━━━━━━━━━━━━━●

    I want to control and manipulate people/ situations to achieve the outcomes I'd like.

    I do not try to control; instead I trust God.

Scripture Memory Verse of the Week

Here is our last verse to ponder, study, and even memorize, if desired. (Remember, all the memory verses are printed out for you in the back of this study guide. You may photocopy them for your convenience.)

So, we are always confident and know that while we are at home in the body we are away from the Lord. For we walk by faith, not by sight.

2 Corinthians 5:6–7 (HCSB)

Also, take a minute now to review all six memory verses. Choose one that you want to make your goal to live out. If you have not already done so, post it in a prominent place where you will see it often. Read it. Ponder it. Memorize it. Live it.

Prayer of Commitment

Close out this study by spending a few moments in prayer. Ask God to continue to guide you as you seek to be a woman after his own heart — a follower who is learning, step-by-step, to stop trying to control and trust him instead. Make this prayer time one of commitment to living life according to his plan for you.

Final Note from the Author

What a joy it has been to walk this road with you as together we learn how to stop running the show and start walking in faith. It isn't easy. Believe me, I know! As a card-carrying member of Control Freaks Anonymous, I have a very difficult time not helping God do his job. However, I know from experience that he is just waiting for us to loosen our grip and learn the thrill of trusting him even in dark times when our sight is severely limited.

My prayer for you is that you too will discover the exhilarating feeling of being a woman who is completely and utterly "out of control" in the most beautiful of ways.

Remember, sister, in order to finally get a grip on life, you have got to decide to *let. it. go.*

Karen

Scripture Memory Verses

For your convenience, the memory verses for this study are printed here. Feel free to photocopy this page and then cut out the verses and place in your purse or post where you can see and study them. Be sure to check to see if any members of your group want to arrive early to the session to practice reciting the verses from memory for each other.

Session 1

Now the serpent was more crafty than any other beast of the field that the LORD God had made. He said to the woman, "Did God actually say ...?" *(Genesis 3:1 ESV)*

Session 2

A [self-confident] fool has no delight in understanding but only in revealing his personal opinions *and* himself.
(Proverbs 18:2 AMP)

Session 3

She opens her mouth with wisdom, and the teaching of kindness is on her tongue.
(Proverbs 31:26 ESV)

Session 4

Truly my soul silently waits for God; from Him comes my salvation. He only is my rock and my salvation; He is my defense; I shall not be greatly moved.
(Psalm 62:1–2 NKJV)

Session 5

For I have learned how to be content (satisfied to the point where I am not disturbed or disquieted) in whatever state I am.
(Philippians 4:11 AMP)

Session 6

So, we are always confident and know that while we are at home in the body we are away from the Lord. For we walk by faith, not by sight. *(2 Corinthians 5:6–7 HCSB)*

About Proverbs 31 Ministries

I f you were inspired by *Let. It. Go.* and desire to deepen your own personal relationship with Jesus Christ, I encourage you to connect with Proverbs 31 Ministries. Proverbs 31 Ministries exists to be a trusted friend who will take you by the hand and walk by your side, leading you one step closer to the heart of God through:

- *Encouragement for Today*, free online daily devotions
- The *P31 Woman* monthly magazine
- Daily radio program
- Books and resources
- Dynamic speakers with life-changing messages
- Online communities
- Gather and Grow groups

To learn more about Proverbs 31 Ministries or to inquire about having Karen Ehman speak at your event:

Call 1-877-P31-HOME
or visit *www.proverbs31.org/speakers/*

Proverbs 31 Ministries
616-G Matthews-Mint Hill Road
Matthews, NC 28105
www.proverbs31.org

Let. It. Go.

How to Stop Running the Show and Start Walking in Faith

Karen Ehman

Many women are wired to control. You're the ones who make sure the house is clean, the meals are prepared, the beds are made, the children are dressed, and everyone gets to work, school, and other activities on time.

But trying to control everything can be exhausting, and it can also cause friction with your friends and family.

This humorous, yet thought-provoking book guides you as you discover for yourself the freedom and reward of living a life "out of control," in which you allow God to be seated in the rightful place in your life. Armed with relevant biblical and current examples (both to emulate and to avoid), doable ideas, new thought patterns, and practical tools to implement, *Let. It. Go.* will gently lead you out of the land of over-control and into a place of quiet trust.

Available in stores and online!

Unglued Participant's Guide with DVD

Making Wise Choices in the Midst of Raw Emotions

Lysa TerKeurst

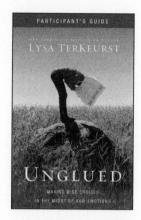

Lysa TerKeurst admits that she, like most women, has experiences where others bump into her happy and she comes emotionally unglued. We stuff, we explode, or react somewhere in between. What do we do with these raw emotions? Is it really possible to make emotions work for us instead of against us? Yes, and in her usual inspiring and practical way, Lysa will show you how. Filled with gut-honest personal examples and biblical teaching, *Unglued* will equip you to:

- Know with confidence how to resolve conflict in your important relationships.
- Find peace in your most difficult relationships as you learn to be honest but kind when offended.
- Identify what type of reactor you are and how to significantly improve your communication.
- Respond with no regrets by managing your tendencies to stuff or explode.
- Gain a deep sense of calm by responding to situations out of your control without acting out of control.

Sessions include:

Session 1: Grace for the Unglued
Session 2: Freedom for the Unglued
Session 3: Four Kinds of Unglued
Session 4: A Procedure Manual for the Unglued
Session 5: Lingering Words for the Unglued
Session 6: Imperfect Progress for the Unglued

Available in stores and online!

Spirit Hunger Workbook with DVD

Filling Our Deep Longing to Connect with God

Gari Meacham

In this six-session video-based study with workbook, author and speaker Gari Meacham identifies the path we share as we struggle to engage God in prayer and belief.

Here, your heart's desire to engage God is unwrapped, and lesser loves are stripped away, until a unique fragrance of God—a scent that has either never been unveiled or has been ignored—is exposed in your heart.

Meacham writes, "With the authenticity of my own life stories—marriage to a professional baseball player, struggles with severe food bondage, and a father who was a quadriplegic—I came to the crisp realization that my prayer life and my level of belief needed to match. *Spirit Hunger* provides a clear path toward matching these heart cries—leading away from crumbs and counterfeit to a hungering for God."

Meacham offers a fresh look on the topic of prayer that will help you move past longings to settle in a place where you can authentically engage God.

This *Spirit Hunger* curriculum pack contains one *Spirit Hunger Workbook* and one *Spirit Hunger* DVD.

Available in stores and online!

Between a Rock and a Grace Place Participant's Guide with DVD

Divine Surprises in the Tight Spots of Life

Carol Kent, Bestselling Author of When I Lay My Isaac Down

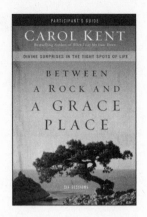

Bestselling author Carol Kent teaches this six-session, video-based study of facing impassable obstacles of life and discovering the last thing you ever expected—the sweet spot of grace.

Join Carol as she teaches the liberating truth that when we are caught between a rock and a hard place, we are given a choice: Will we place ourselves in a posture of humility and complete dependence on God, or will we just "try harder" and stumble over what could be a transforming encounter with grace?

With hope, joy, and a sense of humor, Carol Kent will help you and your group see God's "grace places" in the middle of your worst moments.

Sessions include:

1. Grace in the Hardest of Places—Surprised by Faith
2. Angels in Disguise—Surprised by Mercy
3. Longing for a Better Life—Surprised by Contentment
4. The Secret Power of Gratitude—Surprised by Thanksgiving
5. Why Do You Weep?—Surprised by Joy
6. Dwelling in the Grace Place—Surprised by Freedom

Available in stores and online!

Undaunted Study Guide with DVD

Daring to Do What God Calls You to Do

Christine Caine

In *Undaunted*, Christine Caine, offers life-transforming insights through five inspiring sessions, about how to not only overcome the challenges, wrong turns, and often painful circumstances we all experience, but to actually grow from those experiences and be equipped and empowered.

Using her dramatic life story, Christine Caine takes you on an epic journey through the stages of pain and loss that ultimately lead to hope, healing, transformation, and new beginnings. Along the way, she will show how you pass by miracles every day without realizing it—both in your communities and your lives.

Sessions include:

Session 1: The Call
Session 2: Be the Love
Session 3: Be the Hope
Session 4: Be the Change
Session 5: The Challenge

Available in stores and online!

Share Your Thoughts

With the Author: Your comments will be forwarded to the author when you send them to *zauthor@zondervan.com*.

With Zondervan: Submit your review of this book by writing to *zreview@zondervan.com*.

Free Online Resources at
www.zondervan.com

Zondervan AuthorTracker: Be notified whenever your favorite authors publish new books, go on tour, or post an update about what's happening in their lives at www.zondervan.com/authortracker.

Daily Bible Verses and Devotions: Enrich your life with daily Bible verses or devotions that help you start every morning focused on God. Visit www.zondervan.com/newsletters.

Free Email Publications: Sign up for newsletters on Christian living, academic resources, church ministry, fiction, children's resources, and more. Visit www.zondervan.com/newsletters.

Zondervan Bible Search: Find and compare Bible passages in a variety of translations at www.zondervanbiblesearch.com.

Other Benefits: Register yourself to receive online benefits like coupons and special offers, or to participate in research.

ZONDERVAN®

ZONDERVAN.com/
AUTHORTRACKER
follow your favorite authors